WEIGHT TRAINING FOR MEN

A Beginner's Guide

Kristoph Thompson

Weight Taining for Men - A Beginner's Guide is also available in accessible formats for people with any degree of visual impairment. The large print edition and eBook (with accessibility features enabled) are available from Need2Know. Please let us know if there are any special features you require and we will do our best to accommodate your needs.

First published in Great Britain in 2011 by
Need2Know
Remus House
Coltsfoot Drive
Peterborough
PE2 9BF
Telephone 01733 898103
Fax 01733 313524
www.need2knowbooks.co.uk

Contents

Introduction

Weight training is an essential part of every exercise programme, working
well as a standalone mode of activity, as well as complimenting other forms
of training. It can help you to achieve a number of goals including building
a leaner, stronger physique as well as supporting fat loss. Exactly how
to achieve these results, in a safe and effective way, can be a little more
confusing. There's no shortage of advice around, but it can be difficult and
time-consuming to sift through and work out what's most applicable to you.
This book explains the benefits and basic principles of weight training, helping
you to understand the reasons behind the best route to success, as well as
including three different programmes for you to follow. You can begin training
immediately and will start seeing results in just a few weeks.

First thing's first

- Before you begin, read through the advice and information provided.

- Take your time to understand the fundamentals and principles, as these are
  the foundations for success.

- Take things slowly to begin with, listening to your body and progressing at
  your own pace.

Disclaimer

Exercise is not without its risks, and this or any other exercise programme may result in injury. They include, but are not limited to: risk of injury, aggravation of a pre-existing condition, or adverse effects of over-exertion such as muscle strain, abnormal blood pressure, fainting, disorders of heartbeat, and very rare instances heart attack. To reduce the risk of injury, before beginning this or any exercise programme, please consult a GP or your healthcare provider for appropriate exercise prescription and safety precautions. The exercise instruction and advice presented are in no way intended as a substitute for medical consultation. The author and publisher disclaim any liability from and in connection with this programme. As with any exercise programme, if at any point during your workout you begin to feel faint, dizzy, or have physical discomfort, you should stop immediately and consult a physician.

Chapter One

Why Weight Training?

Benefits of weight training

There are lots of benefits to be gained from regular weight training and the many positive effects can be realised by those of any age. Numerous research articles have shown that the human body responds in essentially the same way to weight training, regardless of age.

Weight loss

Any form of exercise requires extra energy. Energy burned during exercise is measured in calories. Exercise therefore increases your calorie burn. The stored fat in your body can be converted to energy, this process is increased with regular exercise, helping you to reduce stored body fat and therefore lose weight. Exercise not only increases the amount of energy expended during your workout, it also speeds your metabolism (the rate at which your body uses energy) after you've finished exercising. An elevated metabolism means you burn additional calories even while resting. This is known as the 'after burn effect'. This effect lasts longer with weight training than any other form of training, increasing your weight loss potential.

More toned physique

Regular weight training will give you a more toned appearance by reducing your levels of stored body fat and increasing the amount of muscle in your body. Muscle requires a constant supply of energy in order to function. Increasing the size of your muscles will increase your metabolic rate, meaning you burn more calories during everyday activity. The higher your metabolic rate, the easier you should find it to lose weight. Working your muscles with weight training will help you to reduce your levels of body fat and gain a more toned physique even when you're not in the gym.

Increased bone strength and density

Our bone density tends to decrease with age as a result of changes in our diet and the amount of activity we do, as well as slowing in the rate at which new bone is created. This is accepted as part of the ageing process and can lead to conditions such as osteoporosis later in life. Regular weight-bearing exercise, such as weight training, places small amounts of stress on the bones which actually helps to strengthen them over time. During a workout your muscles produce force which they transmit through your bones in order to create movement. This application of force results in microscopic damage to the bones which is repaired as part of the recovery process. The body will overcompensate during this process, leading to stronger, denser bones and a decreased risk of osteoporosis.

Increased self-confidence and self-esteem

Studies have shown that those who exercise regularly tend to report higher levels of self-confidence, and self-esteem, and are generally happier with their own body image. These positive feelings were correlated to the amount and intensity of exercise; the greater the intensity of exercise and the more often it was performed, the greater the level of satisfaction reported. In the short term, exercise promotes the release of feel-good hormones known as endorphins which have been shown to improve mood. Endorphin levels remain elevated after you've finished exercising so the mood-boosting effect stays with you for the remainder of the day.

Reduce the risk of injury

Regular weight training helps to reduce injury by increasing the strength of connective tissue (your ligaments and tendons) and joint stability. Injuries tend to occur when a muscle or tendon is subject to too much force being applied through it, resulting in a tear. Stronger muscles and connective tissue are less

8

prone to injury since they are more capable of handling increased forces. Joint injuries commonly occur when a joint is forced outside its normal range of motion, weight training increases the stability of joints, making them less likely to be moved beyond their normal range.

Immunity and sleep

Those who exercise regularly are less likely to suffer with mild infections and viruses, such as coughs and colds, indicating that exercise promotes a healthy immune system. Be careful though, as too much exercise and insufficient rest/recovery can cause you to become run-down and actually reduce the effectiveness of your immune system. Regular exercise also improves your sleep patterns and since sleep quality and immune function are related, it makes sense that exercise will lead to a more robust immune system.

Increased sports performance

All top level athletes use weight training to increase their performance. Regardless of the event; from the marathon to rugby, weight training can help an individual perform better in their sport. Weight training helps to increase strength and power which is necessary for successful performance in many sports. It helps to correct differences between the left and right side of the body or between different groups of muscles, such as those at the front and rear of the thigh, reducing the overall risk of injury.

These benefits occur as a result of the short and long-term adaptations the body makes to regular weight training. These benefits will only occur if training follows a structure and prescribed set of principles.

Immediate/short-term effects of training

When you do any kind of weight training, the repeated lifting and lowering of the weight causes microscopic damage to the muscle. This damage is different to that which results in an injury, such as a pulled muscle and is, in fact, necessary to bring about the long-term adaptations of training.

Weight training, like any form of physical activity, increases your heart and breathing rate, speeding the rate at which the body uses energy. When lifting weights, the amount of energy burned per minute is comparable to jogging, however this only applies to the time spent performing the movement, not the rest periods in-between sets and exercises. Since exercise increases energy usage, metabolism (the sum of bodily processes that require or produce energy) is raised. With other forms of exercise, such as running or cycling, metabolism returns to normal levels soon after the end of the workout. Weight training causes metabolism to be slightly elevated during the hours following a workout, since energy is needed to fuel the recovery process, helping you to burn additional calories long after your workout is over. This increased calorie burn can help boost weight loss.

Weight training also depletes the stores of energy, know as glycogen, in the working muscles and it can take up to 48 hours for these stores to be restocked. Depleted energy stores are part of the reason why your performance would be impaired if you were to try and do the same workout the following day, which highlights the need for rest and recovery as well as a good diet. For more information on a good, balanced diet see *Food For Health – The Essential Guide* (Need2Know).

Those new to weight training will challenge their body in a way that is unfamiliar, performing moves that require a co-ordinated contraction of lots of different muscles. This co-ordinated contraction may seem tricky at first but quickly becomes familiar as the brain and body work together to master the new movement. In the first few weeks of training the beginner will notice a fairly sharp increase in strength and their ability to complete each workout. This increase stems from adaptations occurring in the system that links the muscle and brain, establishing a stronger connection between both elements. Once the new techniques are mastered, the rate of gain is slowed as the muscles will take slightly longer to adapt to training.

Long-term responses to training

Over a period of months and years the body continues to make adaptations based upon the demands placed upon it by regular weight training. Since each workout results in a slight stress to the body, adaptations are made to ensure that the body can cope with these stresses in future.

The microscopic damage to muscles is repaired, but the body will overcompensate so it is better able to deal with any future demands placed on it. Increases in muscle size, strength and endurance are the results most commonly associated with this overcompensation process.

The same principle of overcompensation occurs with bones and connective tissue (ligaments and tendons). If the muscles become bigger and stronger then the structures they transmit their force through need to also adapt. Resistance exercise increases the density of bones and the thickness of ligaments and tendons. Stronger bones mean that the chances of a fracture are reduced, as well as guarding against osteoporosis later in life. Stronger, thicker ligaments and tendons mean that these structures are also better able to protect against injury.

Increasing the amount of muscle in the body is often associated with a reduction in the amount of stored fat. This effect is often referred to as 'changing body composition' (the proportion of fat and muscle in the body). Since muscle requires small amounts of energy, even when resting, the more muscle a person possesses, the higher their resting energy expenditure. Using weight training to add a little muscle helps you to burn additional calories when resting and doing everyday activities, boosting weight loss.

Weight training will not increase your endurance, for this you need an aerobic activity such as jogging, but it may reduce blood pressure and increase the strength of the heart. A stronger heart is able to pump more blood with each beat, helping to increase its efficiency and reduce the strain of everyday activity.

Principles of training

In order to realise the many benefits of weight training, your training must apply a number of principles otherwise you'll find your results will slow and your efforts will be in vain.

Overload

Training needs to represent a greater stress to the body than previously experienced in order to bring about any meaningful adaptations. Much like you might progress from GCSEs, to A-levels and then on to a degree, with each level becoming increasingly more difficult. In weight training terms this involves trying to lift a slightly heavier weight or doing one more repetition over time. You don't need to apply this principle to each and every workout, but rather over a period of weeks.

Specificity

The body makes adaptations closely related to the demands you place upon it. For example, increases in bone density are specific to the parts of the body involved in training, so doing a leg press exercise will increase the density of the thigh bone, but have no effect on the shoulder. If you have a specific goal in mind, make sure your training is closely linked to this goal. If your goal is to become stronger, the number of sessions per week, exercises per session and weight lifted in each will differ than if your goal was to become more toned and defined because the responses to training are based upon the type of training conducted.

Progression

The body quickly becomes accustomed to the demands you place upon it so in order to increase your fitness you must make sure your training provides a constant challenge. This principle is often referred to as continuous overload as it highlights the need to always challenge yourself.

Reversibility

Unless you continue to make use of the body's adapted state, it will return to its previous condition. For example, if you were to stop training altogether or drastically reduce the intensity you would see a reversal of your progress. Otherwise known as the 'use it or lose it' principle, reversibility highlights the need to continually apply the principles of overload and progression.

Rest/recovery

The adaptations to training occur when you are not exercising so it's very important to build in periods of rest and recovery into your week. Make sure you get plenty of sleep as this is when the majority of adaptations take place. Aim for at least one day of complete rest each week and leave 48 hours between workouts that involve the same muscles. The older you are, or the more intense your training, the longer you will need to recover after each workout. Without adequate rest you will just be running yourself into the ground, stressing the body without allowing it to adapt and compensate. If this occurs, you greatly increase your risk of injury as well and will find it difficult to maintain your current level of training.

Variability

Many training programmes are monotonous, lacking variety or any other kind of change. Since you quickly become accustomed to the training you do on a regular basis, this principle highlights the need to periodically vary the structure and format of your workouts. Small changes made on a regular basis, around every 6-8 weeks, keep your training interesting and help prevent you falling into a training rut. Changing the order of exercises or even the order of workouts in the week should be sufficient, periodically changing the exercises themselves or the equipment used; using a dumbbell instead of a barbell for example, are the sorts of alterations required.

Summing Up

There are many benefits of weight training, these include:

- Weight loss.
- More toned physique.
- Increased bone strength and density.
- Increased self confidence and self esteem.
- Reduce the risk of injury.
- Boosts immunity and sleep.
- Increased sports performance.

In order for these benefits to be realised, training must follow the principles of:

- Overload.
- Progression.
- Reversibility.
- Variability.
- Specificity.
- Rest/recovery.

Weight training results in microscopic damage to the muscles involved. This is a normal part of the training process but differs to the damage caused by an injury. You shouldn't experience any pain during exercise, however mild soreness may be experienced the following day.

Chapter Two

Getting Geared Up

Weight training isn't necessarily something that requires hoards of equipment, in some instances you can use your bodyweight to provide the resistance; doing exercises such as push-ups, chin-ups and single leg squats. A little equipment is recommended to effectively apply all of the principles of training, however this needn't represent a huge financial outlay or take up half the space you have at home.

Joining a gym

Often the only expense is the cost of a gym membership. There can be quite a big difference in fees from one gym to the next, so shop around and ask yourself if you're getting value for money. You don't necessarily need access to the latest equipment, slightly older kit often works just as well as long as it has been properly maintained. Determine if you need all of the bells and whistles of the more expensive gyms, and whether you'd attend the classes or use the pool. If all you need are weights there's often a cheaper, but perfectly functional, alternative.

You'll be visiting the gym regularly so it's wise to pick one that's convenient, close to your home or work for example. Many gyms are part of national or regional chains and will allow you to use other clubs when away from home. This may be beneficial if your job involves a significant amount of travelling, enabling you to stick to your routine throughout the week.

Consider the time of day and even the days of the week that you are planning to work out. Gyms have peak usage times, so it's well worth going along at a time you're most likely to work out to see how busy it will be. There's nothing more frustrating than having to wait to use various pieces of kit, as it can significantly increase your total exercise time without any benefit to you. Peak times tend to be between five and six pm on weekdays. If you aren't planning to visit during peak times then you may be eligible for a cheaper monthly fee, so be sure to ask. It can also be worth finding out how many members there are currently and whether this is set to increase significantly. You wouldn't want to join somewhere because it was quiet and find it overrun with people a couple of months later.

Those new to weight training are advised to use resistance machines as they permit only the prescribed movement. The chest press machine for example, will only allow you to perform that one exercise, so you can be certain you are completing the movement correctly. If you are a beginner it's worth ensuring your gym has one machine for each major muscle group. Free weights (dumbbells and barbells) are recommended for intermediate and advanced trainers as they allow a greater range of exercises to be performed but require a little more co-ordination. Check there is a range of weights available, as well as various racks and bars as you will progress on to using these in a few months, even if you are a beginner.

Other pieces of equipment such as medicine balls and balance trainers are useful to add variety to your training but are not essential pieces of kit. These items can be used to supplement your training, especially as you become more experienced, helping you to vary the challenge you place on your body and apply the principles of variability and progression.

Home gym

You might not want to join a gym, or you might not have access to one in your local area. If this is the case then it's still possible to have an effective workout at home, however you will have to invest in a few basic pieces of kit. As long as you have the space and know you have the self-discipline to train regularly at home then it can save you money in the long run. Even if you were to spend the cost of an annual gym membership on equipment it would be cheaper than the gym from year two onwards.

The essentials

Dumbbells

The best weights for home use are a set of adjustable dumbbells. Dumbbells are essentially hand weights and are one of the most versatile pieces of weight training equipment. The number of exercises that you can do with dumbbells is endless, giving you a huge amount of flexibility in the options available to you.

A gym will have an entire rack of dumbbells of differing weights, often running the length of a wall, which obviously isn't practical for the home. An adjustable set is ideal, requiring minimal storage space yet still enabling you to work on all the different parts of the body. Some muscles are much bigger, and therefore stronger, than others so you need a set of dumbbells that allows you to work different muscle groups. A pair that allows you to adjust from 5-20kg, in 2-2.5kg increments, is ideal as they will be able to accommodate the larger and smaller muscle groups.

Unlike a multi-gym, dumbbells are small so will pack away neatly when not in use. The risk of injury can be slightly higher with free weights as they can move in all directions and require a greater level of stabilisation. Make sure your technique is correct to reduce this risk.

Since dumbbells are often made out of durable metals, it's not unreasonable to expect a good set to last a lifetime, meaning that buying second-hand is a valid option. It's possible to pick up a real bargain from someone who has lost the motivation to train at home, and since there are no moving parts there's not much to go wrong.

Stability ball

You might use a bench in the gym but a stability ball will work just as well, allowing you to do exercises seated or lying supine, such as shoulder presses or chest presses. A stability ball is a large inflatable ball, making it light and easy to store, perfect if space is limited. Doing your exercises on the ball will require you to stabilise to a greater extent, which is great for working on this element of fitness. Be careful when getting yourself in and out of position for each exercise as the ball is likely to move as you do.

You don't need to spend a fortune on a stability ball, cheaper balls often perform as well as the more expensive versions. Balls come in different sizes to accommodate those of different heights. There should be a sizing guide when you buy the ball, but generally speaking your hips and knees should be at right angles when seated on the ball.

Optional extras

Resistance band

Resistance bands are another really versatile piece of kit. Light and very easy to store, resistance bands are essentially large pieces of elastic. These bands can be used to provide extra resistance for just about any exercise. They are colour coded according to tension, so it may be best to buy a couple to give yourself greater flexibility in your choice of exercises. Resistance bands fold up so are perfect if you have a tiny amount of storage space, or want still want to exercise when away from home.

Weightlifting belt

This is a thick leather belt, designed to reduce the chances of a lower back injury. A weightlifting belt is not a necessity but, if you are serious about training this is something to consider when you are lifting heavier weights. Go for one that is 4" wide and buy from a specialist weight training shop.

The belt increases the pressure inside the torso making a more solid platform when you lift, and providing support for the lower back. The belt should be very tight and only worn when lifting. Take the belt off between sets, if you are wearing it throughout your workout then it is too loose and you are not getting the maximum benefit.

Gloves

Again, not a necessity but wearing gloves can help you get a better grip on a weight, as well as preventing the palms of your hands from becoming sore and hardening over time. Leather gloves are best as they are more durable. Some gloves have a wrist strap which can help provide a little extra support for this area if required.

Adjustable bench

A stability ball may not be ideal for lifting heavier weights as it can be difficult to move in and out of position. An adjustable bench will give you the flexibility to perform a range of exercises with dumbbells and barbells. The bench should ideally be able to adjust to a range of angles; both inclined and declined.
A good bench should last a lifetime, so it's worth paying a little more for something sturdy as the cheaper versions can be a little more flimsy in their construction.

Large mirror (to check technique)

Contrary to opinion, this is not to pose in front of between sets! A mirror allows you to check you are performing each rep with correct form and give you visual feedback on where your arms and legs are positioned throughout the movement. As you become more accustomed to the technique involved in each exercise you'll find yourself checking yourself in the mirror and making slight adjustments accordingly. These small adjustments help to ensure you get the most from each set, as well as reducing your risk of injury and preventing imbalances from occurring between the left and right sides of your body.

Summing Up

- Make sure you get value for money from your gym membership, only paying for the facilities you need.

- Check the gym meets all your requirements and isn't going to be too busy at the times you would visit most.

If you are motivated then exercising at home is a viable alternative to the gym. The key pieces of kit include:

- Dumbbells – adjustable from 5-20kg.

- Stability ball.

Optional extras include:

- Resistance band.

- Weightlifting belt.

- Gloves.

- Adjustable bench.

- Large mirror.

Chapter Three

Types of Weight Training

Weight training involves performing movements against some form of resistance, such as dumbbells or barbells, but there are different forms of training, each with their own set of advantages. Knowing which is best, and for what purpose, will help you to decide which type of training will work best for you.

Free weights and resistance machines

One of the most common distinctions between types of training is the mode of equipment used. Free weights are those that aren't fixed and are therefore 'free' to move in any direction. The opposite of this is traditional resistance machines which restrict the user to a pre-defined movement. Both forms of training have their advantages and disadvantages, and one isn't necessarily better than the other. The trick is deciding which will enable you to achieve your goals in the most effective way.

Resistance machines

These tend to be used to perform one movement, a chest press for example, and while they can be adjusted to accommodate different users, the movement is fixed. Resistance machines tend to be recommended for those new to training as there is limited scope for performing the movement incorrectly. This enables the user to be sure they are doing the exercise correctly and reduces the risk of injury.

Machines use a weighted stack, with a pin inserted into this stack, to determine the amount of weight being lifted. The weight stack is attached to a pulley, working against gravity to provide the resistance. Proponents of resistance machines might argue that they are superior to free weights as the weight lifted isn't fixed throughout the movement, as it is with free weights. Each machine is designed specifically around the joints involved in the movement. This means that the amount of weight lifted changes throughout the exercise.

If you were to pick up a 15kg dumbbell and perform a biceps curl, the weight lifted would be 15kg throughout the movement. However, due to the way in which your joints and muscles are arranged, you might be able to lift more weight during the first or last quarter of the movement. The resistance machine changes the weight lifted at different points of the movement according to the strength of the joints involved. In theory this maximises the gains in strength because the muscles are being stressed as much as possible throughout the exercise.

Resistance machines require a lot more space than free weights, and since they usually only permit the user to perform one movement, many are required for a total body workout. For these reasons resistance machines are more practical in a gym rather than at home.

Although risk of injury is reduced with resistance machines, there is still a chance of performing the movement incorrectly due to poor technique or incorrectly setting up the machine. Make sure you familiarise yourself with each machine, seeking guidance from gym staff where necessary. Remember, no two machines are exactly the same so even if they look alike, spend the time getting to grips with how to best adjust them for your body and the specific technique.

Advantages:

- Focuses on one muscle group at a time.
- Goes through a guided and specific range of motion, which can be great when starting strength training or rehabilitating from an injury.
- Assists with control of movement.
- If the machine is properly adjusted it can provide proper form through the lift.

Disadvantages:

- Not well suited to home gyms
- Movements made are not functional, everyday movements.

22

- Focuses on one muscle group at a time. However, during sport and daily living activities we use various muscle groups simultaneously.

- When increasing weight, you must add a whole or half plate (usually approximately 5kg) which may be too large an increase for some individuals.

Free weights

Free weight training involves using dumbbells (weights held in either hand) or barbells (a longer bar with weights affixed either end and held with both hands). Free weights are, by definition, free to move in any direction and have their own devoted following. The free weights area of a gym tends to be associated with the sometimes intimidating bodybuilder-type but that shouldn't be any reason not to include free weight exercises in your programme.

Performing movements with free weights requires the whole body to be stable in order for you to safely complete the move. This develops smaller stabiliser muscles around the body which can actually reduce your risk of injury outside of the gym. Free weight exercises tend to more closely mimic real life movements where you are unsupported when lifting and carrying. Developing these attributes in the gym means you are better equipped to perform these movements outside of the gym when required.

Since the weight is free to travel in any direction, the risk of injury due to incorrect technique is greater. Close attention needs to be paid to technique during each rep in order to prevent injury. If you are unsure about performing any movement then seek guidance from a member of gym staff.

One of the major advantages of free weights is the flexibility in terms of the number of exercises you can perform. It is possible to get a whole body workout with just a set of dumbbells, making them ideal for a home gym. Free weights can also be a time-saver at the gym. At peak times you will most likely have to wait for a certain resistance machines to become free, with free weights all you need is the weight itself and the space to perform the move. The list of possible exercises is enormous, and when you add additional pieces of equipment such as benches and racks, this list only grows in number.

Advantages:

- Can be used at home or at a gym.
- Can perform everyday movements, such as lifts from the floor.
- Increases strength through a full range of motion.
- Requires more co-ordination and control than machine weights, developing these aspects of fitness
- More challenging – it is more difficult to bench press 70kg of free weights than 70kg on a machine press due to machine assistance.

Disadvantages:

- May need a spotter if lifting a heavy weight.
- Knowledge of proper form during the lift is vital for injury prevention.

Hybrids

The concept of resistance training has been around for hundreds of years and the first resistance machines were developed over fifty years ago. During this time many developments have been made that aim to combine the positives of both free weights and resistance machines and minimise the negatives. One simple form of resistance training that incorporates the principles of free weights and resistance machines is the adjustable cable pulley. This is usually two weight stacks with a cable and pulley system attached, set around six feet apart. With this particular piece of equipment it is possible to perform scores of exercises, still challenging the stability of the body and joints but minimising the risk of injury.

Some gyms might also have a versatile piece of equipment known as a Smith machine, particularly one that allows users to move forwards/backwards and up/down. This may be a sound alternative to free weights, particularly for those making the transition from resistance machines to free weights or those with an existing injury.

Functional training

This form of training is designed to prepare the body for the activities performed during daily life. Traditional weight training exercises tend to focus on one set of muscles or involve one movement whereas in daily life we perform a fluid series of movement to complete various everyday tasks.

Functional training may involve machines or free weights, but most commonly requires a greater degree of balance, stabilisation and co-ordination. Functional training exercises are often designed to mimic the everyday tasks, such as picking an object off the floor and placing it in an overhead cupboard. Invariably, exercises are performed standing, as opposed to seated, on a bench, to mimic 'real-life' situations and involve a combination of upper and lower body movement.

Functional training can add variety to your training regime, help you save time as exercises work more than one muscle or set of muscles, and also reduce your risk of injury. Functional training may also be more effective for sports as the movements can be tailored to those performed in the game, developing strength and stability.

Supplemental equipment

The fundamental principles of weight training are essentially the same, regardless of the type of equipment used. These same principles can be applied to additional pieces of equipment to give a well-rounded or altogether more convenient workout.

Kettlebells

Kettlebells resemble a cannonball with a handle and originated in Russia in the early 18th century. Kettlebells are often made of cast iron and come in a range of weights from 2kg up to over 40kg.

The kettlebell is a very versatile piece of equipment, enabling the user to get a total body workout in just a few moves. Just like free weights, the body is required to stabilise and form a solid base for the move and each exercise requires a certain amount of mastery to be performed correctly.

Even though they have been around for hundreds of years, kettlebells have become more popular recently with the upsurge in interest in functional training. Since the traditional kettlebell exercises: the swing, clean and press, and snatch involve lots of different muscles and joints, they make ideal functional fitness tools.

If your gym has kettlebells then certainly include them in your routine, asking for guidance from an instructor so you can master the technique. Exercises involve many different muscles, therefore requiring more energy and helping you to lose weight. If you are looking for a versatile piece of equipment to compliment your home gym then a kettlebell is a useful addition.

Resistance bands

Resistance bands are a very easy way to provide resistance or even assistance in many exercises. Resistance bands are essentially large elastic bands and as such, they are small, light and portable. Bands make the ideal workout tool when you are away from home or on holiday and still want to work out.

Resistance bands come in a variety of thicknesses which determines the amount of resistance they apply, so if you are planning on including them as part of a home or travel gym then decide which exercises you are going to perform and then select the bands that provide the appropriate amount of resistance.

Group weight training

Some gyms offer weight training themed classes which can make a nice addition to your programme. In these classes an instructor guides you through a series of exercises set to music, and you adjust the weight used between each track.

Group exercise is great if you struggle with motivation as you tend to push yourself a little more in a group setting or when an instructor is spurring you on. Beware though, due to the nature of the class, training tends to be higher volume and lower intensity so is better suited to building muscle endurance and toning rather than increasing strength and muscle size.

Devising a training programme

Which exercises and in which order

Generally speaking, you should be doing two or three different exercises for each body part. Identify those areas of the body that you would like to focus on and select exercises that involve these muscles. Exercises should be slightly different so as to stress the muscles in a slightly different way. Your choice of exercises should be based upon your training experience and your goals, as well as the equipment available. Be sure you stick to exercises your are familiar with, seeking guidance if you are unsure.

Your exercises should be completed in a certain order, moving from large to small muscles, those that involve more than one joint to those that involve just one, and from those that are higher in complexity to lower complexity.

For example, a lower body workout might consist of the following exercises:

■ Leg extension.

■ Lunges.

■ Leg press.

■ Leg curl.

■ Calf raises.

According to the principle outlined above, the exercises should be completed in the following order: lunges, leg press, leg extension, leg curl, calf raises. Completing the exercises in this order follows the principles outlined above. The larger muscles of the thigh and hip are worked first before moving on to exercises that work the rear of the thigh and calf. Lunges and the leg press involve the hip, knee and ankle joints so are completed first, whereas the leg extension, leg curl and calf raise involve only one joint so should be completed in the latter stages of the workout.

Ordering the exercises in this manner helps you to perform to your fullest and therefore get the most out of each session. Exercises with complex techniques, or that require a high level of balance and co-ordination should be completed at the start of the session before you are fatigued. These exercises require a greater level of concentration and stress the small stabiliser muscles around the involved joints. Smaller muscles tire more quickly than larger muscles so performing exercises that heavily involve smaller muscles later in the session increases the risk of injury and reduces the effectiveness of the exercise.

How much/how long – sets and reps

One movement, consisting of the lifting and lowering phase of the exercise is referred to as one repetition, or rep. A series of repetitions performed consecutively is known as a set. Reps and sets are the weightlifting equivalent of time or distance and are how the volume of training is assigned.

Your training volume is dictated by your training goal (e.g. getting stronger or improving muscle tone). Each rep should be performed slowly and under control, with proper form.

How often should I train?

You shouldn't train the same muscles more than three times a week, leaving at least 48 hours between each workout. The number of times you train each muscle will depend on the number of sets and reps in each workout. The total number of workouts per week will therefore depend on how your training is split up; if you were to complete a whole body workout with four sets for each body part then twice or three times a week would be sufficient. If you were to complete one workout for each body part, performing 12-16 sets, for each then you might work out five or six days a week, doing a different body part each day.

Rest and the importance of recovery

The training session itself represents a stress to the body and actually results in microscopic tears to the muscle fibres. These tiny tears are different to a muscle injury and are a necessary part of the training process. The body detects this slight level of damage and repairs, yet as part of a protective mechanism it will overcompensate and it is this process that explains how the body adapts to training.

It is crucial therefore, that in order to bring about the adaptations you are striving for, you allow sufficient rest and recovery between sessions. It is during the rest and recovery periods that the body adapts, rather than in the gym itself, training only serves as the impetus that prompts these adaptations. Without adequate rest and recovery your body does not have the opportunity to repair and regenerate prior to the next session. In this situation the risk of injury increases significantly and results plateau. You should therefore allow 48 hours between workouts that involve the same muscles, and have a week of planned recovery where you do light exercise in place of your regular sessions every 6-8 weeks.

Training for different goals

It is possible to plan your training according to the specific aims of your programme. Whether you wish to add muscle tone, to get a little stronger or to build muscle, the process of selecting exercises and their order remains the same. The major difference exists in the amount of sets and reps of each exercise you perform.

As a general rule the following guidelines should be followed:

Goal	Sets	Reps	Rest between sets
Toning/muscle endurance	2-3	12-15	30-45secs
Building muscle	3-4	6-12	60-90secs
Strength	4-6	2-6	2-3mins

You should select a weight that allows you to complete the required amount of repetitions in each set, and no more. Initially, this may require a little trial and error. Remember, the lifting and lowering phases of each rep should be performed slowly and under control to maximise benefits and reduce the risk of injury. You should adjust the weight for the subsequent set if you are unable to complete the previous set, or feel you could have completed more repetitions.

Reviewing your training programme

You'd be surprised just how quickly your body adapts to the challenge your weight training programme presents. In order to continue to progress towards your weight training goals, you should increase the challenge to force the body to continually adapt.

It is recommended you review your programme every six to eight weeks, making a number of changes that increase the challenge to your body. These changes need only be small, not necessitating a complete overhaul of your programme, as you will need to make these changes on a regular basis.

One of the easiest changes is to increase the intensity by increasing weights used for each exercise; 3-5% is an average increase. You may still be able to perform the same amount of reps and sets as previously, indicating that you have made positive adaptations, otherwise adjust the volume of training by either increasing or decreasing the amount of reps and sets.

If possible, you might adjust the order of exercises, yet still following the guidelines for exercise order outlined previously. When doing this, try to increase the weight you lift in the exercises you now perform earlier in your workout, while trying to keep the weights of the exercises you now complete later in the session the same.

You can also change the exercises themselves, substituting a free weight exercise for a resistance machine or vice versa, or a set of dumbbells for a barbell. Again, these need not be drastic changes, even a slight variation is sufficient to bring about adaptations.

Summing Up

- Resistance machines tend to be recommended for beginners, whereas free weights are more appropriate for intermediate or advanced weight trainers.

- Certain types of machines represent a 'best of both' concept, such as an adjustable cable pulley.

- Functional training prepares you for day-to-day tasks and invariably involves the whole body, making it a real time-saver.

- Kettlebells, resistance bands, and group weight training offer slightly different alternatives to free weights and resistance machines and can be used to vary your training.

- One movement or lift is referred to as a 'repetition'. A number of consecutive repetitions is known as a 'set'.

- You shouldn't train the same muscles more than three times a week, leaving at least 48 hours between each workout.

- Adaptations take place between workouts so rest/recovery is crucial.

- The number of sets and reps depends on your training goal – toning, building muscle etc.

- Make small changes to your programme every six to eight weeks.

Chapter Four

Foundation Programme – Weight Loss and Toning

Weight training can be used to achieve many goals, including weight loss and toning muscles. The distinction between different training goals is made via the manipulation of the training volume (reps and sets), and the training intensity (the weights lifted). To increase muscle tone and aid weight loss, a higher volume of training at a more moderate intensity is performed, as compared to training for increased muscle size or strength.

The most effective means of bringing about weight loss through training is to involve the largest muscles as these will result in a greater amount of energy being expended during the workout. Regularly training these muscles will significantly increase your calorie expenditure, helping you to lose weight.

This workout is designed to work each of the major muscles of the body and should be performed three times a week. Complete each workout in a circuit-style, doing one set each exercise consecutively to complete one circuit. Perform three circuits in total during each workout. Spend six weeks doing this programme before moving on to the next.

It is important to complete each exercise with good form, as even when using resistance machines there is the potential for injury. Pay attention to your breathing, inhaling during the lowering phase and exhaling during the lifting phase of each movement. Breathing in this manner not only reminds you to breathe when training, but also creates a more stable base from which to apply force from. When you breathe out, the pressure inside your chest cavity increases which means that your torso becomes firmer. This increases your overall stability, providing more support and reducing the chances of injury.

If the exercise requires you to use a weight, select one than allows you to complete 15 repetitions with good technique and no more. If you are able to complete more than 15 repetitions, the weight is too light and you won't be applying the principle of overload. If you are unable to complete 15 repetitions, reduce the weight as by performing fewer reps, you are shifting the focus of your training away from toning towards increasing muscle size and strength. Adjust the weight for each circuit depending on how you felt during one before.

When using resistance machines don't allow the weight plates to make contact with those on the stack – the movement should be silent. To get the most from each rep your muscles should be under constant tension during the lifting and lowering phases. When the weight plates bounce off one another slack develops in the cable attached to the weight plate. At this point muscle tension ceases momentarily, reducing the total amount of work performed by the muscles. When the slack is taken up again the muscle must start producing force again very quickly which increases the risk of an injury at this point. Bouncing the weight in this manner generates momentum and reduces the work of the muscles. The weight is too heavy if you have to bounce it in order to move it.

Warm-Up

Begin with the cardio and mobility exercises described in chapter 9.

Exercises

Ball wall squat

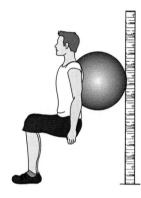

Place a stability ball against a wall and rest against it, facing away from the wall so your lower back is supported. Take a step forwards so your feet are just in front of the rest of your body. Your feet should be hip-width apart and facing forwards, hands on hips.

Slowly squat down, bending your hips and knees and allowing the ball to roll up your back. Stop when your hips and knees are bent at 90 degrees. In this position your shin should be vertical and your knees over your ankles. You may have to adjust your foot position to achieve this.

Push through your heels, straightening your legs and return to the starting position without locking your knees and then repeat. Hold a dumbbell in each hand if you can comfortably perform 15 repetitions of this exercise with your bodyweight alone.

Leg curl

Set up the machine, adjusting the seat back so that your knee is aligned with the pivot point of the machine when seated. Adjust the foot pad so the backs of your ankles are in contact with the pad with legs straight. Your hips, knees, and ankles should be in alignment.

Bring the thigh pad down to rest securely on top of your thighs. Hold the handles loosely, bending your knees, taking your feet under the seat without moving your upper leg.

Return your legs to the starting position with control, without locking your knees and repeat. Don't allow your back to come away from the seat at any time.

Calf raise

Begin standing with the balls of your feet on a step and drop your heels off the back. Holding a dumbbell in your right hand, grip the rail or wall with your left for support.

Keeping your back straight, rise up onto your tiptoes, then lower down slowly and repeat.

Pulldown

Adjust the thigh pad so that when seated your legs are held firmly in place with the pad resting on mid-thighs. Take hold of handle with palms facing away, outside of shoulder width, ensuring they are evenly spaced.

Sit with your thighs under the pad, your chest up and back straight. Pull the bar down to touch the top of your chest (under control), without arching your back. Straighten your arms, without locking your elbows and repeat.

Chest press

Set the machine so the handles are in line and level with mid-chest. Keeping your knuckles in line with your forearms, straighten your arms without locking your elbows. Return slowly to the starting position and repeat. Keep your back in contact with the seat and feet firmly on the floor throughout.

Shoulder Press

Set the seat height so the handles are level with shoulders when seated. Take hold of the handles so palms face away.

Keeping your back in contact with the seat and feet flat on the floor, press upwards, straightening your arms without locking your elbows.

Lower your hands so they are level with your ears and repeat.

Bench dips

Set up two flat benches slightly further than your legs' length apart and parallel to each other. Sit with hands resting on the edge of the bench either side of your hips. Place both feet on the other bench and bend your elbows slightly.

Keeping your torso upright and elbows pointing backwards, lower yourself towards the floor until your elbows are bent at 90 degrees.

Straighten your arms and return to the start. Place a weights plate on your thighs if you can comfortably complete 15 repetitions using just your bodyweight.

Seated curls

Adjust a bench so the back is upright. Sit with your back against the backrest and feet firmly on the floor. Take hold of a dumbbell in each hand with palms facing each other, arms straight by your sides.

Bend both elbows, bringing the dumbbells towards your shoulders, turning your wrists on the way up so your palms face upwards. Your upper arm should stay still throughout this movement.

Lower your hands slowly to the start, turning the palms to face each other on the way down and repeat.

Crunches

Lie on your back with feet flat on the floor, hips and knees bent, hands lightly touching your temples or across your chest.

Slowly lift your head and shoulders a few inches off the floor, tightening your stomach. Lower back to the start and repeat.

Keep the distance between your chin and chest constant throughout the exercise

Need2Know

Cool down stretches

Finish your workout by completing the following stretches, holding each at the point of mild discomfort for 20 seconds.

Chest

1. Stand with your back straight, looking straight ahead. Place both hands on the back of your head, elbows out to your side. Exhale and slowly bring your elbows back. You should feel a stretch across the front of your body.

Shoulders

2. Take one arm across your chest, taking hold with the other forearm. Exhale, pulling your upper arm in towards your chest. Keep your whole body facing forwards throughout. You should feel a stretch across the back of your shoulder. Repeat with the other arm.

Triceps

3. Take one arm straight up, then bend your elbow so your forearm points straight down the centre of your back. Take hold of your elbow with the other hand and pull gently towards your head. You should feel the stretch at the back of your upper arm. Repeat with the other arm.

Upper back and biceps

4. Interlock your fingers and turn your palms to face towards you. Raise your hands up to shoulder height and push forwards slightly. You should feel a stretch across the back of your body.

Calf

5. Begin facing a wall then step forwards with your left foot, placing your hands on the wall with arms straight. Slowly bend your left knee, pushing your right heel into the floor. Hold. Bend your right knee and keep your heel in the floor (hold for 8-10 seconds). Repeat on the other side. You should feel the stretch in your lower leg.

Quads

6. Using a wall to steady yourself if necessary, bend one knee, lifting the foot towards your bottom and taking hold with the hand around the foot. Keep your legs together and knees in line, pushing your hip forwards. You should feel a stretch in the front of your thigh. Repeat with your other leg.

Hamstrings

7. Step one foot forwards and keeping it straight lift your toes. Bend the other knee slightly. Lean forwards from the hips, keeping your back straight and chest up, with your hands resting against the front of your standing leg. You should feel a stretch in the back of your thigh. Repeat with your other leg.

40

Summing Up

■ Weight training that involves the largest muscle groups is best for weight loss.

■ Complete the programme three times a week in a circuit-style, doing one set each exercise consecutively to complete one circuit.

■ Perform three circuits in total during each workout.

■ Spend six weeks doing this programme before moving on to the next.

■ Pay attention to your breathing, inhaling during the lowering phase and exhaling during the lifting phase of each movement.

■ Select a weight that allows you to complete 15 repetitions with good technique and no more. If you are able to complete more than 15 repetitions, the weight is too light. If you are unable to complete 15 repetitions, reduce the weight.

■ When using resistance machines, don't allow the weight plates to make contact with those on the stack – the movement should be silent.

Chapter Five

Intermediate Programme – Increase Strength and Build Muscle

This workout is designed to increase strength and build muscle. In order to achieve these goals, training volume (sets and reps) is reduced and the intensity of training (weight lifted) increases as compared to the foundation programme. The exercises are split up into three workouts, each being completed once a week and targeting a different set of muscles. Each workout will stress and fatigue the sets of muscles, with the repair and adaptation process taking place during the week of recovery between each of these sessions.

A combination of free weight and resistance machine exercises are included. Perform each exercise with good form, ensuring your body positioning is correct and each movement is completed slowly and with control. Apply the same breathing principles as in the foundation programme; inhaling during the lowering phase and exhaling during the lifting portion of each exercise. Complete each rep without jerking the weight or contorting your body to generate momentum or gain additional leverage. If you find this occurring, stop immediately and reduce the weight for any subsequent sets.

Complete the programme in a 12-week cycle. Perform three sets of 12 repetitions of each exercise for the first three weeks, resting for one minute between sets and exercises. For weeks four, five and six increase the weight you are lifting slightly and perform three sets of 10 reps, with the same rest period. Perform four sets of 8 reps for weeks 7-9, increasing the rest period between sets to 90 seconds; and four sets of 6 reps for weeks 10-12, again with 90 seconds of rest between each set. Each time you reduce the number of reps in each set, you should increase the weight slightly. Follow the same principles as in the previous programme, completing each move slowly and under control.

Warm-up and cool-down

Begin each workout with the same warm-up as described in chapter 9. End each workout with the stretches detailed in chapter 4.

Workout 1 – chest and triceps

Bench press

Use a bench press rack and set the bar so when lying on the bench, gripping the bar, there is a slight bend in your elbow. Lie on the bench so that your eyes are level with the bar then take hold of the bar with hands evenly spaced just outside shoulder width. Straighten your arms, lifting the bar off the rack and taking it forwards slightly so it is above your mid-chest, keeping your wrists strong.

Inhale and lower the bar to your chest, your forearms should point straight upwards at this stage (if not, re-rack the bar and adjust your hand position). Pause momentarily then drive the bar upwards, straightening your arms without locking your elbows. Lower and repeat.

Ensure you keep your feet firmly in contact with the floor, without lifting your back or hips off the bench.

Incline press

Set up an adjustable bench so it is inclined at around 30 degrees. Stand just in front of the bench facing away, holding a dumbbell in each hand. Rest the bottom end of each dumbbell on your lower thighs then sit down on the bench so the dumbbells are now resting on your thighs.

Sit back, lifting your legs as you do so, taking the dumbbells level with, and just outside, mid-chest, then plant your feet firmly on the floor. This is the starting position.

Inhale, then exhale and push the dumbbells upwards, straightening your arms without locking your elbows. Your arms should be vertical at this stage. Lower the dumbbells to the starting position and repeat.

Ensure you keep your feet firmly in contact with the floor, without lifting your back or hips off the bench.

Dumbbell flyes

Begin lying on your back on a flat bench holding a dumbbell in each hand with a slight bend in your elbow, palms facing each other, hands above your chest.

Maintaining the slight bend in your elbow, arc your arms out so your hands are now level with your shoulders. Pause momentarily then return to the starting position and repeat.

Ensure you keep your feet firmly in contact with the floor, without lifting your back or hips off the bench.

Lying extensions

Begin lying on a bench holding a barbell with hands shoulder-width apart directly above your shoulders. Without moving your upper arms, bend your elbows and bring your hands to just above your forehead.

Straighten your arms and return to the starting position.

Pushdowns

Using one side of an adjustable pulley machine, attach the straight bar attachment to the highest point and take hold with your hands shoulder-width apart. Bring your hands down level with your chest, your elbows tucked against your sides.

Straighten your elbows without moving your upper arms or bending forwards from the hips. Pause momentarily then slowly return to the start and repeat.

Workout 2 – Back and biceps

Pull-ups

Begin standing underneath the pull-up bar then step or jump up, taking hold with your hands 1.5 times shoulder width apart, palms facing away from you.

Pull your chest up level with your hands, then lower slowly down again, straightening your arms and repeat.

Place a dumbbell between your legs, or use a weighted belt to increase the difficulty if required. However, if you cannot complete the prescribed amount of reps then switch to a chin-up (hands shoulder-width, palms facing towards you) or use an assisted pull-up machine.

Single arm row

Place a dumbbell to the right of a flat bench. Place your left knee and hand on the bench with your right foot to the side of the bench. Take hold of the dumbbell with your palm facing towards you, your right arm straight with back flat.

Pull the dumbbell up towards the side of your ribcage, bending your elbow and keeping your upper arm close to your side. Do not rotate your torso as you lift the weight. Lower the dumbbell, straightening your arm and then repeat.

Reverse grip pulldowns

Adjust the thigh pad so that when seated your legs are held firmly in place with the pad resting against your mid-thighs. Take hold of the bar with palms towards you, shoulder-width apart, ensuring they are evenly spaced.

Sit, with your thighs under the pad, with your chest up and back straight. Pull the bar down to touch the top of your chest (under control), without arching your back. Straighten your arms, without locking your elbows and repeat.

Preacher curl

Sit on preacher bench with the back of your arms against the angled pad. The seat should be adjusted to allow the armpit to rest on top of the pad. Take hold of an EZ or angled bar with hands shoulder-width apart, palms facing upwards. Bend your elbows, bringing your hands towards your shoulders. Lower the bar back to the start and repeat. The back of your upper arm should remain in contact with the pad throughout the movement.

Hammer curl

Begin standing, holding a dumbbell in each hand with your palms facing inwards. Keeping your upper arms against your sides, raise one dumbbell bringing your hands towards your shoulder. Lower to the starting position and repeat with the other arm.

Workout 3 – Legs and shoulders

Squat

Set up a barbell on a squat rack just below shoulder height. Step underneath the bar with your feet shoulder-width apart and the bar resting across your upper back. Take hold of the bar with hands evenly spaced outside your shoulders, your elbows bent to less than 90 degrees.

Straighten your legs, lifting the bar out of the rack, and step back to clear the supports.

Keeping your back straight, chest up, and looking ahead, simultaneously bend your hips and knees, as if you were going to sit on a chair.

Your bottom will move backwards and your weight should be towards your heels.

Squat down until your hips are just higher than your knees. Push through your heels and return to standing, without locking your knees and then repeat.

Keep your heels flat on the floor, breathing in at the top of the movement and breathing out as you drive the bar upwards.

Leg press

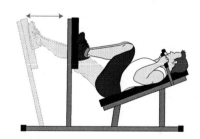

Place your feet hip-width apart on the foot plate, with your knees in line with your toes.

Slowly bend your hips and knees to 90 degrees, keeping your back in contact with the seat back.

Push through your heels, straightening your legs without locking your knees. Return to the start and repeat.

Leg extension

Sit on the machine with the seat back adjusted so it is in contact with your back and with your knee aligned with pivot point of the machine.

Adjust the foot pad so your lower leg makes contact with the pad just above the ankle, and your knees bent to less than 90 degrees.

Take hold of the handles and straighten your legs, without locking your knees, then slowly return to the starting position and repeat.
Don't allow your back to come away from the seat at any time.

Stiff legged deadlift

Begin standing holding a barbell with your hands evenly spaced just outside your thighs with knees slightly bent.

Bend forwards from the hips, keeping the bar close to your legs, your back straight and chest out, lowering the bar to mid-shin level.

Straighten your hips and return to the start then repeat.

Calf raise

Begin standing with the balls of your feet on a bench or step, your heels over the edge, holding a dumbbell in your right hand. Place your left arm against something for balance should you need it. Lower your heels below your toes to feel a slight stretch in the calf, then come up onto your tiptoes, slowly lower and repeat.

Cool-down stretches

Finish your workout with the stretches described in chapter 4.

Summing Up

- Each workout targets a different set of muscles and should be completed once a week.

- Perform each exercise with good form, ensuring your body positioning is correct and each movement is completed slowly and with control.

- Complete each rep without jerking the weight or contorting your body to generate momentum or gain additional leverage.

- Complete the programme in a 12-week cycle. Perform three sets of 12 repetitions of each exercise for the first three weeks, resting for one minute between sets and exercises.

- For weeks four, five and six increase the weight you are lifting slightly and perform three sets of 10 reps, with the same rest period.

- Perform four sets of 8 reps for weeks 7-9, increasing the rest period between sets to 90 seconds; and four sets of 6 reps for weeks 10-12, again with 90 seconds of rest between each set.

Chapter Six

Strength and Sport

This workout is designed to build upon the strength and endurance gained from the previous two programmes. The aim of this programme is to further increase strength and bring about adaptations that will enhance your sporting performance. The training volume and intensity are essentially unchanged from the previous programme since the goal remains strength-orientated.

The programme predominantly utilises free weights that will challenge your muscles as well as your balance and co-ordination. By increasing these components of fitness you will be developing your functional strength which will directly benefit your sport. Some exercises require you to move your limbs independently, helping to correct any strength deficits between the right and left sides of your body. This has a direct translation to sports as you are often required to perform unilateral movements, such as throwing, hitting or kicking.

As before, the programme is split into three workouts, with each being completed once a week. The programme is based upon a 10-week cycle, starting with three sets of 10 repetitions for two weeks, then three sets of eight reps for four weeks, and finally four sets of six reps for another four weeks.

Apply the same principles as in the previous programmes, focusing on proper technique, breathing and body alignment. During the standing exercises, ensure you complete each move from a stable base with your feet hip-width apart, knees soft and stomach muscles engaged. This position enables the optimum transfer of force from the lower to upper body, an essential component of a range of sporting activities.

Warm-up and cool-down

Begin with the cardio and mobility exercises described in chapter 9. Finish each workout with the stretches detailed in chapter 4.

Workout 1

Push press

Stand with your feet hip-width apart, holding a barbell level with your shoulders.

Bend your knees slightly, keeping your torso upright, then quickly straighten your knees, coming onto your tiptoes and pressing the bar straight up, landing softly with knees slightly bent.

Straighten your knees then repeat.

Dumbbell press

Begin lying on a bench with your feet firmly planted on the floor, holding a dumbbell in each hand level with your chest, your palms facing towards your knees. Slowly press the dumbbells upwards, straightening your arms without locking your elbows. Lower to the start and repeat.

Standing cable flyes

Stand in the centre of a dual adjustable pulley machine with the handles set to level with your shoulders (if possible), otherwise use the highest fixed attachment. Take hold of the handles and take a step forwards, with your hands slightly behind your chest and elbows slightly bent – this is the starting position. Keeping your torso upright, bring your hands together to meet in the centre in an arcing motion, without bending or straightening your elbows, and taking one hand over the other. Slowly return to the start and repeat. Alternate the top hand with each set.

Need2Know

Dips

Take hold of a set of parallel bars that are approximately shoulder-width apart. Step or jump up so your arms are straight, supporting your bodyweight – this is the starting position. Keeping your torso upright, bend your arms to around 90 degrees, keeping your wrists strong. Straighten your arms to return to the start and repeat.

Woodchopper

Stand side-on to the cable stack, with a rope attachment on the pulley. Keep a fairly wide stance, with arms straight and abs tight. Exhale and pull the rope out in front of you and across the body in an arc, finishing with hands around knee level, legs slightly bent and weight transferred to the far leg. Complete one set then repeat on the other side. Make the movement explosive as you rotate down, control as you release the weight back up and then repeat.

Plank supermans

Begin in a plank position, upper body resting on forearms, your body in a straight line from head to toes. Without letting your hips sag, extend your left arm straight out and lift your right foot off the floor slightly.

Hold for a count of one then lower down and do the same with the other arm and leg – this is one rep. Continue, alternating sides to complete one set.

Workout 2

Deadlift

Stand in front of a barbell with feet shoulder-width apart, toes pointing straight forwards.

Take hold of the bar just outside your shins with an alternated grip (one palm facing towards you, one facing away).

Squat down so your hips are lower than your shoulders. Your back should be flat or arched but not rounded, with shoulders over or just in front of the bar, looking straight ahead. This is the start position.

Inhale and as you exhale, lift the bar from the floor, without letting the hips rise before the shoulders. Keep your back flat and arms straight, with the bar close to your shins.

As the bar rises above the knees, move the hips forward to move the thighs against the bar. Continue to straighten the hips and knees until standing upright.

Lower the bar back to the starting position, slowly bending the hips and knees and keeping your back flat. Repeat, allowing the bar to come to a complete stop on the floor and not letting it bounce to start the next rep.

Barbell row

Stand with feet hip-width apart holding a barbell with hands outside hips, palms facing towards you. Bend your knees slightly and bend forwards from the hips so your torso is at around a 45 degree angle to the floor, keeping your back flat.

Pull the bar towards your lower chest, without allowing your torso to move or rounding your back, lower slowly and repeat.

Need2Know

One-legged squat and row

Place a single handle on a low pulley
machine. Take hold with your right hand
and take a couple of steps back so there
is tension in the cable when your arm is
straight. Transfer your weight to your left leg
and lift your right foot off the floor slightly.
Keeping your back straight, squat down so
your left hip is slightly higher than your knee.
Push through your heel and straighten your
leg, bringing your right hand in towards your
body and right knee level with your hips.
Squat down again, straightening your arm,
and repeat.

Alternate shoulder press

Begin standing with a dumbbell held in
each hand level with your chin, your knees
soft and back straight. Press your right
hand straight upwards, straightening your
arm. Lower slowly and repeat with your left
arm. Continue, alternating arms.

Lateral raise

Begin standing holding a dumbbell in
each hand, with your elbows slightly bent
and palms facing towards each other. Take
your arms out to the sides, so your hands
are level with your shoulders, keeping your
elbows slightly bent and your upper body
still. Lower slowly to the start and repeat.

Workout 3

Step up

Stand in front of a step roughly 30cm high, holding a dumbbell in each hand, then place the whole of your right foot on the step.

Push through your right heel and step up, bringing your left leg onto the step without leaning your upper body forwards.

Step down and repeat to complete one set.
Change legs for the next set.

Lunge

Stand with your feet hip-width apart, holding a dumbbell in each hand. Take a large step forwards with your right foot then bend your hips and knees simultaneously, lunging down until your back knee is just above the floor. Your torso should be kept upright, your front shin almost vertical with knee behind your toes and in line with your ankle. Push through the front foot and bring your feet back together. Repeat, stepping forwards with the left foot. Alternate the front foot with each rep.

RDL (Romanian deadlift)

Stand with feet hip-width apart, holding a barbell with hands outside your hips, palms facing towards you with knees slightly bent. Bend forwards from the hips, keeping your back straight and chest up, moving the bar down your thighs and shins as you do so. Stop when the bar reaches mid-shin level, then slowly return to the start and repeat.

Need2Know

One-legged calf raise

Begin standing with the balls on your feet on a step, your heels dropped off the back, holding a dumbbell in your right hand, gripping the rail or wall with your left for support. Shift your weight to your left leg then lift your right foot and place it behind your left.

Keeping your back straight, rise up onto your tiptoes, then lower down slowly and repeat.

Curls

Begin standing, holding a dumbbell in each hand with palms facing inwards. Keeping your upper arms against your sides, bend your right arm, curling the dumbbell towards your shoulder, rotating your forearm as you do so, so your palm faces towards you. Lower to the starting position and repeat with the other arm. Continue, alternating sides to complete one set.

Crunch with twist on the ball

Lie on your back on a stability ball with your hips and knees bent, feet flat on the floor, hands lightly touching your temples.

Slowly lift your shoulders off the floor and twist your upper body to the left, taking your right shoulder towards your left knee. Lower yourself back down and repeat, twisting to the right. Continue, alternating sides to complete one set.

Cool-down stretches

Finish your workout with the stretches described in chapter 4.

Summing Up

■ The aim of the programme is to further increase strength and bring about adaptations that will enhance your sporting performance.

■ The programme will challenge your muscles as well as your balance and co-ordination.

■ The programme is split into three workouts, with each being completed once a week.

■ The programme is based upon a 10-week cycle, starting with three sets of 10 repetitions for two weeks, then three sets of eight reps for 4 weeks, and finally four sets of 6 reps for another four weeks.

■ Focus on proper technique, breathing and body alignment during each movement.

Chapter Seven

Breaking Through Plateaus

Why training can stagnate

In order to keep making progress and seeing results, your training should adhere to the principles of overload (training should represent a greater stress to the body than it is usually accustomed) and progression (demands of training should increase gradually over time). In theory, you should continually make progress, however it's not uncommon to experience periods where you stop seeing results, and this is referred to as a 'plateau'.

Failure to apply the principles of training

Plateaus occur for a variety of reasons but the most common cause is that the two principles above are not fully applied. The mechanism by which the body adapts to training further highlights the need to apply these two key principles. Without sufficient stress to the systems of the body, no training adaptations will occur.

Your body can quickly adapt to the demands you place upon it, so what once was challenging can soon be completed with ease. If the training programme fails to progress, the body isn't further challenged into responding. This means no positive adaptations will be made and training/results will stagnate.

Loss of motivation

A plateau can be caused by a dip in motivation which results in a subconscious reduction in effort levels. If you are completing your programme each week with less enthusiasm than when you first started you won't be pushing yourself to apply the principle of overload. You are in a sense doing the same workout week in and week out. Your results will slow or stop because the body doesn't need to make further adaptations to complete this workout. Lack of results can lead to further losses in motivation with one effect compounding the other.

No real programme structure

Taking a whimsical approach to training and flitting from one exercise to the next is a sure-fire way of bringing about a plateau. If your programme doesn't have any kind of structure then the challenge it represents to the body is highly inconsistent. Some weeks you may overload too much, whilst at other times you may not be causing sufficient stress to bring about adaptations. Without a relatively consistent level of overload, your progress will halt and you'll stop seeing results.

Lack of knowledge and understanding

Often, the demands of a programme are sufficient to start with, but when the initial adaptations have been made the programme should adapt with you, to ensure you continually challenge yourself. Without an understanding of how to make subtle adjustments to the programme as a whole, then you will reach a point where your results will stagnate. The knowledge required isn't colossal, a basic understanding of how to manipulate training intensity and volume, as well as a knowledge of a range of exercises, is sufficient.

Insufficient rest/recovery

Thus far the importance of continually overloading the body has been stressed, however if this were relentless, without allowing sufficient rest and recovery, it would inevitably lead to a plateau. As highlighted in a chapter 2, the positive adaptations occur between training sessions. If the next training session begins before adequate recovery has occurred the body literally runs itself into the ground as the diagrams below illustrates.

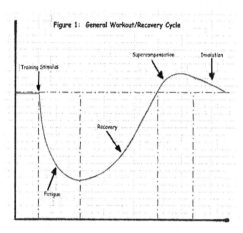

Figure 1: General Workout/Recovery Cycle

Following a training session the body is fatigued and needs time to recover. The positive adaptations are made during recovery and overcompensate for the demands of training, resulting in an improvement in fitness.

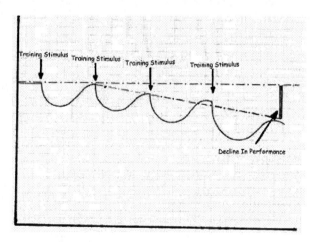

With insufficient rest between sessions the body doesn't have a chance to recover before the next training session starts. The session begins with the body already in a fatigued state and the overcompensation mechanism doesn't have the opportunity to take effect.

This phenomenon, referred to as overtraining, is associated with lots of additional negative effects, including a significantly increased risk of injury and illness. In order to prevent overtraining you should allow 48 hours between training sessions that work the same part of the body, as well as planning a rest (or active recovery) week every 8-10 weeks of training.

The importance of variety

Doing exactly the same thing every session will prevent you from meeting your goals because you won't be making any progress. It may also increase the risk of an overuse injury as the same muscles are used again and again. It is recommended that you make small changes to your workout every six to eight weeks in order to keep exercise varied.

Small changes help you to apply the principles of overload and progression which are necessary for the reasons outlined above. Without variety your training can quickly become monotonous and your enthusiasm will wane. In this situation you'll find it more difficult to motivate yourself to train, and to push yourself during each session.

In order to keep progressing you need to allow sufficient time for the body to physically recover and adapt, but to also keep psychologically motivated. By varying your training every six to eight weeks you can view it as a series of training blocks, with the aim of making as much progress as you can during each block. After each block, a week of active rest or recovery will help you to physically and mentally recharge in preparation for the next block of training.

Practical techniques to avoid stagnation

Understanding motivation

Motivation is the secret of a successful exercise programme. It's the reason we begin an exercise programme full of zeal, and yet it also explains why we can go weeks without working out. As a rule, motivation is temporary and we need to approach all endeavours with this is mind. It is a feeling and like all feelings, it comes and goes. Understanding how and why we become motivated will ensure you keep training week after week.

Many things impact on achieving our fitness goals but a consistent level of motivation is really important. At the most difficult moment, when you're feeling flat, tired and your results aren't coming as fast as you had hoped, motivation is what will keep you getting out of bed early, going to the gym and pushing on through.

Whilst you might dread your sessions to start with, there's no denying that working out actually makes you feel good. Exercise triggers the release of endorphins, feel-good hormones that are responsible for the 'exercise high' you experience after your workout and in the hours that follow. As you progress through your programme you will also find your energy levels increasing, your stress levels decreasing and over time you will come to associate exercise with something that makes you feel great. Motivation increases with enjoyment, so the sooner you start looking forward to an exercise session the easier it will be to work out.

Whilst motivation comes relatively easily to begin with, it tends to decrease with time. Typically we are able to hold our attention to a goal for no more than 1-3 weeks. If we are not seeing significant results after this time, we really start to struggle with our motivational levels. It's after a month then that you need to focus on staying motivated.

Extrinsic or intrinsic motivation

Get to the bottom of why you want to exercise. If you are motivated by an outside factor, such as your partner wanting you to tone up, this is called extrinsic motivation. If your motivation comes from wanting to do something for yourself, such as improving your energy levels, this is intrinsic motivation. An extrinsic factor may be enough to get you started and give you that initial push to start training, but to continue to achieving your goals, motivation needs to be intrinsic.

Importance of assessing/recording progress

Regularly monitoring and charting your progress gives you some form of feedback which can help to keep you motivated. Seeing yourself move closer towards your goals can spur you on to keep training. Without any kind of feedback you will not know if your training is having any tangible effect and you can easily become disinterested. If you ever feel your motivation slipping you can use the results of your assessments to show how much progress you've made, helping to get you back on track.

Once you have set your training goals, regularly assessing your progress against these goals is the best way to check you are on course to achieving them. You may find that you need to make small changes in certain areas because you are not on course. Without this feedback you will have no real way of knowing how you are progressing.

Means of assessment

There are a number of different means of assessment and your chosen method should be based on your specific goals. An explanation of each method is given below:

- Bodyweight – taken first thing in the morning, once a week, using the same set of scales to give an indication of weight loss/gain.

- Circumferences – the distance measured around various parts of the body to indicate weight loss/muscle gain in specific areas of the body.

- Chest – taken around the nipple line.

- Mid-abdominal – taken level with the belly button.

- Hips – taken around the widest point of the buttocks when viewed from the side.

- Thigh – taken directly below the fold of the buttock on the right thigh.

- Upper arm – taken halfway between the armpit and crease of the elbow of the right arm.

- 5RM – the maximum amount of weight that can be lifted for five repetitions with proper form. For use with multi-joint exercises only.

- 10RM – the maximum amount of weight that can be lifted for ten repetitions with proper form. For use with single-joint exercises.

- Bodyweight squats – the number of bodyweight squats you can perform in one minute. Feet are placed approximately shoulder-width apart, hands across chest. Bending your hips and knees to 90 degrees and returning to standing counts as one rep.

- Press-ups – the number of full press-ups you can perform in one minute with proper form, lowering your chest to just above the floor.

- Sit-ups – the number of full sit-ups you can perform in one minute with hands across your chest, bringing your shoulders up towards your knees.

- Resting heart rate – Sit or lie quietly for at least 5 minutes and then take your pulse at your wrist or your neck for one minute, counting each beat.

Goal	Measures
Weight loss	bodyweight, circumferences
Muscle tone	circumferences, bodyweight squats, press-ups and sit-ups
Strength	5 and 10RM
Weight gain	bodyweight, circumferences
Overall health/fitness	bodyweight, circumferences, resting heart rate

How often

The relevant tests should be taken before you start training to give you an idea of your starting point, and then repeated every 10-12 weeks. You may find that your goals change during the year. If this is the case, you should adapt the tests you conduct. For example, you may complete a block of training to increase muscle tone, in which case you should complete the appropriate tests prior to starting this new block to get an idea of your baseline levels and then again at the end to assess your progress.

Always conduct the tests at the same time of day to enable you to make the most meaningful comparisons at any given time. Bodyweight and circumference readings are best taken first thing in the morning on an empty stomach to minimise the effect of any food or drink you have consumed during the course of a day. The volume of food and fluids in the body at a given time, as well as other factors, can affect bodyweight by up to seven pounds.

The effects of one test can also affect your performance in any subsequent tests. For example the push-up test may affect your performance in the sit-up test. To make sure you can compare your results directly, perform the tests in the same order each time, allowing the same rest periods between each.

Interpreting results

The main reason to conduct these tests is to chart your progress and to check that you are actually moving closer to your fitness goals. In these instances you will be comparing one set of results with one(s) recorded previously. In general, it is likely that the initial improvements will be fairly significant whereas others may be slower to respond. Strength, for example, might noticeably improve during the first 4-6 weeks. This increase can be explained by a greater mastery of the techniques involved rather than any changes to the muscles themselves. This improvement will slow as further increases in strength are a result of muscular adaptations which occur from around week six onwards.

In general, the longer you have been training the smaller the gains you make between each bout of testing. The closer you are to your optimal performance level (often genetically pre-determined) the more difficult it is to improve significantly. Weight loss, for example, tends to slow the closer you get to your ideal weight. Consider the case of an elite sprinter, when they first start training they might see an improvement of half a second during a year of training, whereas when they reach their peak they might be aiming for an improvement of a few hundredths of a second. When you first start training you might improve your push-up scores by 15% but after a year or so you might only increase this by one or two repetitions between periods of testing. This is to be expected and shouldn't be a source of disheartenment, as long as you are seeing an improvement then your training is correct.

Tips to stay motivated

- Set goals – a mixture of short and long-term goals will help give your training focus and you'll feel a sense of achievement each time one is met, helping you to stay motivated.

- Log it – keep a record of each workout, noting down sets, reps, weights and even how you felt before, during and after. Refer to this training log whenever you feel disheartened, to remind yourself how much progress you've made.

- Learn to be flexible – it's better to train on days when you can give 100% rather than a token effort. As long as you are completing your weekly quota of sessions, there is no need to feel guilty if you just can't bring yourself to train on a particular day.

- Adapt your plan – be ready to adapt your programme to fit in with your circumstances. If you've had to work late and there's no longer enough time for your hour-long workout, complete a high intensity 20-minute workout instead.

- Recruit a training partner – training partners are a great way to increase/ maintain motivation in respect of achieving fitness goals. Two heads are better than one in suggesting new ideas, as well as making training a more social experience.

Summing Up

- A stagnation of results, known as a plateau, can occur for a variety of reasons, the most common being; failure to apply the principles of training, loss of motivation, no real programme structure, lack of knowledge and understanding, insufficient rest/recovery.

- Doing exactly the same thing every session will prevent you from meeting your goals and may also increase the risk of an overuse injury. It is recommended that you make small changes to your workout every six to eight weeks in order to keep exercise varied.

- Extrinsic motivators are outside factors whereas intrinsic motivators are things from within you. An extrinsic factor may be enough to get you started and give you that initial push to start training, but to continue to achieving your goals, motivation needs to be intrinsic.

- Regularly monitoring and charting your progress gives you some form of feedback which can help to keep you motivated.

- There are a number of different means of assessment including; bodyweight, circumferences, strength testing, muscular endurance tests and resting heart rate. These tests should be repeated every 10-12 weeks.

- In order to stay motivated try setting goals, keep track of your results/progress, be flexible and ready to adapt your plan, and train with a partner.

Chapter Eight

Nutrition

Weight training helps to build or tone muscle, but in order for this to take place the body requires the materials to do so. These materials are provided by the diet in the form of the food groups carbohydrate, protein and fat. These foods are broken in a process called metabolism to provide energy and the building blocks for growth, repair and all other essential daily functions. Following a number of nutritional principles will help to keep your diet on track.

Nutritional principles for weight training

Vary your diet

Every food contains different nutrients in differing quantities. By eating a variety of foods you ensure the body gets all of the nutrients in the quantities it requires to be healthy. If you stick to the same foods in your diet, or cut out one of the main food groups altogether you will miss out on the valuable nutrients contained within.

Eat enough carbohydrate

Carbohydrates, or 'carbs,' are the body's preferred source of energy during exercise, especially during weight training where shorter bouts of intense exercise are performed. Some may shy away from carbs, thinking that they will make them fat when in reality, carbs are needed to fuel muscle growth and help the body to burn fat.

Consume enough calories

All food contains energy which is measured in calories. If you consume insufficient calories you lack the energy needed to fuel your body for training. Since you need to train hard to overload your body and provide the stimulus for adaptations, as well as fuel the recovery process, a low calorie diet will prevent you from meeting your weight training goals.

Eat regularly

Forget the 'three square meals a day' adage; active people must fuel themselves throughout the day. This means eating small meals and snacks every few hours. This doesn't necessarily involve eating more calories, just spreading these calories over a greater number of meals. Eating regularly increases metabolism and the body's ability to process nutrients, as well as stimulating fat burning and reducing appetite.

Energy intake

The exact amount of energy and each individual nutrient required depends on many factors including your age, how hard and often you train, your training goals and the demands of your daily life.

Energy is measured in calories, both in terms of the amount consumed from food and those expended during the day. The concept of weight loss or gain works like a set of balance scales. If more calories are consumed than expended any excess energy is stored as fat and weight increases. If more calories are expended than consumed, stored fat is used to provide the additional energy and weight loss occurs. When calorie intake and expenditure are equal, bodyweight remains the same.

A general rule for calorie intake is to consume between 32 and 40 calories per kilogram of bodyweight. Calorie intake should be higher for those whose daily life is more active and those who exercise more regularly and at a higher intensity. If your daily life is less active and you don't perform any additional forms of exercise, your calorie intake should be towards the lower end of the recommended range.

Energy from food comes from three sources; carbohydrate, protein and fat. A combination of these three food groups provides all of the energy needed complete daily activities and exercise as well as to fuel the recovery process.

Protein

Protein is the food most commonly associated with weight training but more protein doesn't necessarily mean more muscle. The amount of protein in most diets is usually sufficient and actually exceeds the recommended intake of 0.8g per kg of bodyweight for non-exercisers.

Your protein intake will depend on your training goal. For those wanting to build muscle, 1.6g per kg of bodyweight is recommended. If you take part in regular aerobic exercise you may well need a little extra protein so 1.8g per kg of bodyweight is recommended.

Protein can be used as a source of fuel during aerobic exercise, particularly when carbohydrate stores run low. Protein is made up of a number of amino acids, one of which can be converted into carbohydrate and used for energy. When carbohydrate is limited the body can break down stored protein (muscle) for energy, causing a loss of muscle mass over a prolonged period.

1.6-1.8g of protein per kg of bodyweight may also be appropriate for those using weight training to cut body fat since this process involves reducing calorie intake. Increasing protein intake during this time aims to prevent the loss of muscle via the conversion to energy.

Carbohydrate

Carbohydrate should make up the majority of your daily calorie intake, ranging from 50-60% of total calories. Individual carbohydrate intake can be calculated based on bodyweight, with 7-9g per kg being consumed daily.

Carbohydrate provides the body with a ready supply of energy which is stored in the muscles and liver to be utilised when required. Carbs can be divided broadly into two categories, simple and complex, based upon their structure.

Simple sugars, found in cakes and chocolate, require little or no digestion and can be used by the body very quickly. These types of sugar should be kept to a minimum as they cause a rapid increase in blood sugar levels, followed by a sharp drop. This rise and fall in blood sugar can bring a period of vigour followed by a feeling of lethargy which increases the likelihood of snacking between meals.

Complex carbs, such as brown rice, have a more intricate chemical structure and take longer for the body to break down. These types of carbohydrate are recommended as they release their energy slowly over the course of hours and keep blood sugars levels relatively constant. Eating plenty of complex carbs avoids the rapid fluctuations in blood sugar levels and keeps your energy levels steady throughout the day.

Fat

Normally associated with weight gain and blocked arteries, excess calories are converted to fat and stored in the body, regardless of their source, helping to give fat its bad name. Fat, however, is an integral part of the diet, performing many essential functions. Gram for gram, fat contains more than twice the amount of energy of protein and carbohydrate, providing the fuel for everyday activities. Stores of fat are broken down and converted into a usable source of energy during low intensity activity, with even the leanest individual having an enormous amount of stored energy.

Fat from food comes in three different kinds; saturated, monounsaturated and polyunsaturated. Saturated fat is solid at room temperature and tends to come from animal sources, such as cheese and butter. Polyunsaturated and monounsaturated fats tend to be liquid at room temperature and come from nut, vegetable or seed sources. Polyunsaturated fats are found in soybean oil, corn oil, safflower oil, fatty fish, and some varieties of nuts and seeds. Sources of monounsaturated fats include olive oil, avocado, and cashew nuts.

Too much fat in the diet can cause weight gain and the related health problems. In particular, too much saturated fat in the diet can increase cholesterol. Conversely, eating more unsaturated fat can lower cholesterol. Generally, it is recommended that no more than 30% of your total calories come from fat, with saturated fat accounting for no more than 10% of daily calories. If you are trying to stay lean you should lower your fat intake to 20% of total daily calories, cutting saturated fat to 5%.

Tips to reduce fat

■ Replace saturated fats like butter and lard, with small amounts of unsaturated fats such as olive oil, rapeseed oil, sunflower or corn oil.

■ A grilled chicken breast without the skin contains a third less saturated fat than with skin. Remove the skin of any white meat and trim off any visible fat from other meats too.

■ Use semi-skimmed, 1% or skimmed milk rather than whole or condensed milk. Swapping a 200ml glass of full fat milk for semi-skimmed milk cuts your saturated fat intake by 2.9g.

■ Use nutrition labels on packaging to help you choose the foods lowest in fat and saturated fat. There should be no more than 3g of fat per 100g for a product to be low in fat and fewer than 1.5g of saturated fat for it to be low in saturates.

■ Grill, bake, steam, boil or poach foods rather than frying in oil. A portion of cod fried in batter has 2.9g of saturated fat and 445 calories, but an average portion of baked cod has just 0.4g of saturated fat and only 115 calories.

■ Use a spray or teaspoon to add oil when cooking, with a good pan you might be surprised at how little you need to use.

Fuelling your workout

What, when and how much you eat before exercise can significantly affect your performance. Getting the right balance of these variables can make the difference between feeling full of energy and enthusiasm, and feeling flat and lethargic during your workout.

Ideally you should eat between 2 and 4 hours before you workout, leaving enough time for the food to be digested but not too long so you begin to feel hungry again. The timing of your pre-exercise meal will depend on your own personal preference, daily schedule and the time of day you plan to train. If you leave too long an interval between eating and training, your blood sugar levels may drop which can affect your performance, leave you feeling tired and increase your risk of injury. Training with steady blood sugar levels will enable you to train harder and for longer.

Since you will be mostly burning carbohydrate during your workout you should aim to start with your stores of carbs fully stocked. Your pre-exercise meal therefore should be moderately high in carbs with a little fat and protein. The Glycaemic Index, or GI, is a rating of how quickly a carbohydrate source results in a rise in blood sugar levels and can be used to shape your choice of food for this meal. Low GI foods provide a steady release of energy and are recommended. Good pre-workout meals include:

- Rice with chicken and salad.

- Jacket potato with tuna, beans and coleslaw.

- Wholemeal sandwich with chicken, fish or egg and salad.

A pre-workout snack 1-2 hours before exercise can help to top-up blood sugar levels and ensure your energy levels don't drop during your workout. A small amount of moderate GI carbs, such as a piece of fruit, yoghurt or a cereal bar is recommended.

Speeding recovery between sessions

Nutritionally, the most important thing after exercise is to re-stock your stores of carbohydrate and provide the protein building blocks to repair and adapt. The best time to start refuelling is immediately after exercise, as the uptake of nutrients is faster during this period than at any other time. Your carbohydrate stores are re-stocked in three phases. Firstly, during the first two hours after exercise replenishment is most rapid, approximately one and a half times the normal rate. Secondly, during the subsequent four hours the rate slows but remains higher than normal. Thirdly, uptake returns to normal levels after this period.

Consuming carbohydrate and protein immediately after exercise takes advantage of the 'window of opportunity' of nutrient uptake during the first two hours. Research has shown that delaying eating until after this period significantly delays the recovery process. 1g of carbs and 0.5g of protein per kg of bodyweight are recommended immediately after exercise. High GI carbs are best as they are more rapidly absorbed by the body than low GI sources.

A small meal consumed around 2 hours after exercise will ensure that the body can draw upon sufficient supplies of energy to repair. This meal should contain a moderate amount of carbohydrate, with a little protein and fat. Resting during the post-exercise period will also help speed recovery as your overall demand for energy is reduced.

Supplements

There are countless supplements marketed to offer a multitude of benefits from weight loss to increased strength. The sports supplement market has grown significantly in recent years and supplement use is much more commonplace today. With so many products on offer, knowing which will be of most benefit can be difficult.

With regard to weight training, two supplements stand out in terms of having the greatest scientific body of evidence espousing their use; protein and creatine.

Protein

Since muscles are made of protein and weight training can increase your daily protein requirements, it figures that a protein supplement might be of benefit. There's no rule that your protein should come from supplements, some may relish the chicken for breakfast, lunch and dinner approach but for convenience and speed of absorption a protein shake is definitely worth considering.

A post-workout protein shake (with some added carbs) is one of the best ways of taking advantage of the 'refuelling window' since liquid-based nutrients require less digestion and therefore can be absorbed by the body more quickly than solid food. It can also be more convenient than cooking and storing a meal to consume immediately after your workout.

Choosing a protein powder can be tricky and your first port of call should be the nutritional information table on the label. If a protein powder seems too cheap to be true then the chances are it contains as much sugar as it does protein. Sugar is inexpensive so is often used as a filler ingredient, adding extra calories and reducing the total protein content. If extra calories are what you're after then a mass gainer supplement which contains a mix of carbs and protein would be a good fit. If stocking up on protein alone is your goal then a supplement with protein as the main nutrient is a must.

Types of protein

To further confuse matters there are different sources of protein. Whey protein is the most widely available and a good bet. Things aren't so straightforward however, as you then have the choice of isolate, concentrate, blended or hydrolysate.

Whey isolate tends to be more expensive as it has a higher biological value (the proportion that is absorbed by the body) and on the whole contains less fat than whey concentrate. Whether it's worth the extra money is debatable but most powders tend to consist of a blend of the two anyway, creating a happy medium.

In whey hydrolysate powder the proteins have been partially pre-digested so they are more readily absorbed by the body. Beware though – this does give it a very distinct taste which may not to be to your liking. Hydrolysate is a 'next generation' protein with some promising research behind it so it might be worth trying if you know you've got a strong stomach.

Whey protein has been shown to be broken down and absorbed by the body more quickly than casein based protein. This isn't a bad thing, but depends on what you need it to do. Immediately after a workout, whey protein makes the most sense since it is absorbed quickly. As a protein meal replacement, or just before bed, casein may be more appropriate because it releases protein more slowly into the bloodstream.

Creatine

Creatine is a naturally occurring substance, produced in the liver and kidneys and found in certain foods, such as red meat. Creatine has consistently been shown to result in increases in strength and muscle mass during periods of training.

Creatine is particularly beneficial to weight training as it is turned into a tiny unit of energy, creatine phosphate. This is the fuel used for the initial 10 seconds of activity, roughly the duration of each weight training set. Between sets these stores of energy are replenished and an increased amount of creatine phosphate stored in the muscles results in an enhanced ability to recover between bouts of intense activity. An enhanced recovery capacity during exercise allows you to perform more total work during training as you are better able to recover between sets.

Creatine usually comes in powdered form and a larger, loading dose is suggested for around seven days to increase muscle stores. After this point a smaller maintenance dose will be sufficient to keep stores elevated.

Increasing the dosage above the recommended amount will not convey additional benefits. The body has a ceiling on the amount of creatine it will store in the muscles. If this is exceeded, the excess will be excreted from the body.

Meal timings

Throughout the day

- Drink fluids regularly, at least 2 litres of water should be consumed during the day.
- Never skip breakfast as this helps keep metabolism elevated, provides energy for the morning's activities and prevents snacking later in the day.
- Small meals/snacks should be spaced every few hours to keep metabolism elevated.

Before exercise

- Consume at least 250ml of fluid before exercise.
- Eat around 4 hours before exercise to allow food to be digested.

- Snack around 30-90 minutes before your workout to provide additional energy. This should contain around 250kcals, made up of mostly carbs with a little protein.

During exercise

- Sip water every 15-20 minutes to prevent dehydration.

After exercise

- Weigh yourself before and after exercise and replace every 500g of weight lost with 750ml of water.

- Consume 1g per kg of bodyweight of carbs and 0.5g per kg of protein within 30 minutes after exercise to help kick start the recovery process.

- Eat a small meal 2 hours after exercise containing a mixture of carbs and protein.

Summing Up

■ More protein doesn't equate to more muscle. Most diets tend to exceed the recommended protein intake so you may not need to add a huge amount to your diet.

■ Carbohydrate should make up the majority of your daily calorie intake, ranging from fifty to sixty percent of total calories. Individual carbohydrate intake can be calculated based on bodyweight, with 7-9g per kg being consumed daily.

■ Generally, it is recommended that no more than 30% of your total calories come from fat, with saturated fat accounting for no more than 10% of daily calories. If you are trying to stay lean you should lower your fat intake to 20% of total daily calories, cutting saturated fat to 5%.

■ Try to eat between 2 and 4 hours before you workout, leaving enough time for the food to be digested but not too long so you begin to feel hungry again.

■ Consuming carbohydrate and protein immediately after exercise takes advantage of the 'window of opportunity' of nutrient uptake during the first two hours.

■ Lots of nutritional supplements are marketed towards weight trainers but the two with the greatest body of scientific evidence supporting their use are protein and creatine.

Chapter Nine

Supplemental Forms of Training and Injury Prevention

Progress towards your goals is dependent on the application of the principles of overload and progression. The same type(s) of training week in and week out will ultimately lead to a plateau of results and the onset of boredom. Having an awareness of a variety of different methods of training will help you to keep your workouts varied and continually enhance your performance.

Stretching/Flexibility

Being able to touch your toes doesn't seem to have the same appeal as being bigger or stronger so this aspect of fitness is often overlooked. In truth, becoming more flexible can help you to become bigger and stronger by making you more effective at performing different exercises and reducing your risk of injury so you can train uninterrupted.

There are two different kinds of stretching; maintenance and developmental. Maintenance stretching is designed to maintain your current level of flexibility. This type of stretching usually takes place at the end of your workout as part of your cool-down. Weight training can make your muscles and tendons feel tight, thus reducing your flexibility in the days following training. Maintenance stretching after your workout can help to reduce the sensation of tight muscles and help you to recover more quickly after a hard workout. Maintenance stretching involves holding a stretch at the point of mild discomfort for 20-30 seconds. After your workout you should include a stretch for each of the muscles that you have just trained.

Developmental stretching aims to increase your flexibility and works on the same principles as weight training. You perform sets of stretches, trying to do more (or reach further) than you did in the previous set or session.

Increasing your flexibility increases the range of motion around a joint which can benefit you in three ways. Firstly, being more flexible allows you to perform an exercise with a greater range of motion. A greater range of motion results in the involvement of more muscle fibres, and therefore a greater training stimulus. For example, increasing your hip flexibility allows you to go lower into a squat position and involve more of your hip extensor muscles. The more muscles that are involved the greater the calorie burn and the amount of weight you can lift, both of which lead to more significant progress towards your goals. Secondly, a more flexible joint is more resistant to injury as injuries often occur when a muscle or tendon is taken beyond its comfortable range of motion. If, through training, you have increased your comfortable range of movement you reduce the likelihood of an injury through over-extension of a joint. Finally, being more flexible can improve your sporting performance. Consider the example of a golf swing, if you are more flexible in your shoulders and back you can take the club further back in the backswing. The greater the backswing, the greater the club head speed on impact with the ball, and the further the ball will travel. To use developmental stretching to increase your flexibility try three sets of 30 seconds of each stretch, aiming to stretch a little further with each set.

Prehab

The old saying 'an ounce of prevention is worth a pound of cure' can be directly applied to weight training. Spending a little time injury-proofing yourself is a small price to pay when compared against the amount of time you would need to take off training if you were to suffer an injury. The reversibility or 'use it or lose it' principle of training states that when training ceases, any adaptations start to slowly reverse. This means that all your hard work is undone while you recover, making an injury very frustrating.

There are various steps you can take to lessen the chances of an injury, such as increasing your flexibility by doing developmental stretches or thoroughly warming up prior to exercise. In addition, performing a number of strengthening exercises once a week can help to prevent injuries. Injuries tend to occur during exercise when fatigue sets in and technique changes slightly. Slight changes in technique can shift the workload to other muscles which can cause them to be overstressed. Increasing the endurance of larger muscles as well as increasing joint stability by working on the smaller muscles will help to prevent injury.

Shoulder

A team of small muscles help to keep the shoulder stable during movement. Weakness or fatigue in these muscles during sport/activity can contribute to a shoulder injury.

Standing rotations – 2x25 reps

Begin with your shoulders at 90 degrees, forearms pointing straight down to the floor, holding a pair of light dumbbells (no more than 3kg). Keeping your upper arm level and without rocking your torso, rotate your shoulder and bring your hand up so your palm faces forward.

Inward shoulder rotations – 20 reps each arm

Attach one end of a dyna-band to a door knob and take hold of the other end with your right hand, your elbow bent at 90 degrees and arm rotated so your forearm points towards the door handle. There should be a small amount of tension in the band at this point.

Keeping your elbow by your side, rotate your arm inwards so your forearm rests across your stomach.

Slowly return to the start and repeat.

Outward shoulder rotations – 20 reps each arm

Attach one end of a dyna-band to a door knob and take hold of the other end with your right hand, your elbow bent at 90 degrees and arm rotated inwards so your forearm rests across your stomach and towards the door handle. There should be a small amount of tension in the band at this point.

Keeping your elbow by your side, rotate your arm outwards so forearm points to your right. Slowly return to the start and repeat.

Wall slides – 10-15 reps

Begin standing with your back resting against a wall, your feet around a foot and a half from the wall. Raise your arms up level with your shoulders then bend your elbows to 90 degrees, keeping your arms pressed against the wall. Press your lower back into the wall. This is your starting position.

Slowly raise your hands upwards, straightening your arms then return to the starting position.

Hamstrings and lower back

Hamstring drop – 3x5 reps

This simple exercise helps to strengthen the hamstrings and prevent strain, in addition to strengthening exercises make sure you regularly stretch the muscle as tight hamstrings can cause you to round your back during lifting movements, increasing risk of injury.

Begin kneeling with a partner supporting your feet. Slowly lower yourself to the floor, using your hamstrings to control the movement. Push back up to the start with your arms and repeat. Try to keep your body in a straight line from knees to shoulders, without bending forwards at the hips.

Glutes and core

Single-leg bridge – 2x20-30 seconds each leg

Helping to strengthen the glutes and core muscles will keep the hip stable and you off the sidelines.

Begin as if you were about to do a sit-up, with your arms resting on the floor by your sides. Tighten your stomach and glutes, and lift your hips off the floor so there is a straight line between knees and shoulders – hold in this position. Lift your right leg off the floor and straighten your leg – hold in this position before lowering and repeating on the other leg. Try to keep both hips perfectly level at all times.

Balance/stability

Injuries during training and everyday activity can occur when a joint or muscle is stretched beyond its normal limits, or too much force is applied through it. Correcting a body position that could potentially result in an injury requires a combination of the awareness of where your body is positioned as well as the strength and power to change this position. Balance and stability training will improve these abilities, reducing the likelihood of an injury occurring.

You don't necessarily need to perform specific exercises to improve your balance and stability. Completing exercises from your existing programme seated or lying on a stability ball can be sufficient. A stability ball creates a slightly unstable surface which requires your stabiliser muscles to contract in order to maintain your body position. Regularly including unstable surfaces training in your workouts will encourage you to be more aware of your body position and increase your sense of body awareness, as well as the strength/ endurance of your stabiliser muscles. You don't necessarily need to use any additional equipment, try performing conventional exercises such as biceps curls or shoulder presses with one leg slightly raised.

Safety guidelines

Warming up (plus sample warm-up)

A warm-up helps to prepare you physically and mentally for your workout, not only helping to reduce the risk of injury and post-workout soreness, but also increase your performance. The warm-up serves to bridge the gap between your resting and exercise state by gradually increasing your heart rate and body temperature, as well as helping to loosen muscles. A weight training warm-up should consist of a number of different phases; an aerobic phase, mobility phase and training-specific phase.

Aerobic phase – perform some kind of aerobic activity involving the upper and lower body, such as rowing or jogging, for at least 5mins. Start at a lower intensity and gradually increase this as you progress. The aerobic phase helps to increase blood flow to the working muscles, increasing their temperature in order to prepare them for the next phase of the warm-up and the workout as a whole.

Mobility phase – the goal here is to loosen the joints by moving them through their range of motion. Start with a slower, smaller movement and increase this with each repetition until you are moving through the full range of motion at speed. The mobility phase should be performed after the aerobic phase as the muscles respond best when already warm. Your muscles can be likened to a piece of chewing gum, when cold they are easier to tear but when warm they are much more malleable.

Training-specific phase – here you perform the exercise with a very light weight, or even no weight at all to help establish the brain-body connection. This serves as a form of mental rehearsal and any repetitions you perform in this phase do not count towards the 'working sets' of your workout. Aim to complete 2 or 3 warm-up sets, gradually increasing the weight lifted in each until you reach the weight you had planned to lift for the first working set of your session.

Sample Warm-up

Aerobic Phase

Use the scale below to adjust your intensity during each minute according to the table.

Time (min)	RPE
0-1	6-8
1-2	8-9
2-3	9-10
3-4	11-13
4-5	9-6

Borg Scale of Perceived Exertion		
6	Very, very light	How you feel when lying in bed or sitting in a chair relaxed.
7		
8	Very light	Little or no effort.
9		
10		
11	Fairly light	Target range: How you should feel with exercise or activity.
12		
13	Somewhat hard	
14	Hard	
15		
16	Very hard	How you felt with the hardest work you have ever done.
17		
18	Very, very hard	
19		
20	Maximum effort	Don't work this hard!

• TeleRehab™ Advantage Cardiopulmonary Monitoring System
• NICORE™ External Counterpulsation (ECP) Therapy System

ScottCare Corporation
4791 West 150th Street
Cleveland, Ohio 44135
A Scott Fetzer, Berkshire Hathaway Company

Phone: 800-243-9016, ext. 116
Fax: 216-201-6130
www.scottcare.com

ScottCare

Mobility phase

Neck rotations – look over your right shoulder, then drop your chin to your chest and slowly rotate your head around to look over your left shoulder, then slowly back to the centre and to your right. Complete 8 rotations.

Shoulder rolls – lift your shoulders forwards and up towards your ears, then roll them back and down. Complete 8 backward rotations, and then 8 forward rotations.

Shoulder circles – take your arms out to your sides and make small circles in one direction, gradually increasing the size of the circles with each rep until your upper arms brush your ears. Complete 10 rotations in each direction.

Trunk rotations – begin standing with your hands on your hips then turn to look over your right shoulder, turning your upper body rather than just your head. Turn back to the centre and then to the left. Increase the speed of the movement with each rep, releasing your arms and allowing them to turn with you. Complete 8 rotations in each direction.

Heel kicks – begin standing then bend your right knee, bringing your heel up towards your backside. Straighten your leg and repeat on the other side. Complete 8 kicks on each leg.

Leg swings – stand side-on to a wall and place your hand against it. Lift one leg and swing it forwards and back, increasing the height of the swing with each repetition. Keep your upper body upright throughout. Complete 8 repetitions on each leg

Training-specific phase

Perform two or three sets of your first exercise, increasing the weight with each set. Perform each rep slowly with good form.

Common causes of injuries and staying injury free

Some may regard injuries as a part of weight training, just like they are a part of sports. In fact, injuries shouldn't have to be that common because weight training takes place in a controlled environment, whereas sports take place in a constantly evolving environment. You are (or should be) in control of each aspect of every lift, and if this is the case then the risk of injury is minimal. That said, there are certain factors which increase the risk of injury:

Incorrect technique

The most common weight training injuries are related to poor technique. Perform an exercise with bad technique and it can instantly result in an injury. Your body is designed to move in a certain way, and specific exercises are performed to develop the muscles responsible for this movement. Correct technique is the most important element in bringing about gains in training. This is much more important than simply moving the weight from start to finish position by any means necessary. Twisting, turning and contorting your body while moving the weight to gain extra leverage only increases your risk of injury. Recognising when your technique begins to deteriorate during a set and correcting or stopping at this point is crucial to staying injury free.

Too much weight

If you can't perform the movement with strict technique, if you can't control it when you lower it, or if you have to jerk or heave the weight in order to lift it, then the weight is too heavy. Many different structures must work together in order to produce the movement required to lift a weight. These structures form a chain consisting of the muscle, tendon, ligament, and joint. This chain is only as strong as its weakest link. If an individual component is stressed beyond its limits through lifting too heavy a weight, an injury will occur.

Training too often

Not allowing sufficient recovery between workouts is known as overtraining and this state negatively impacts your ability to train and adapt. Continuing to exercise in this state sees the quality of your training decline as you struggle to maintain your current level of performance. Your technique and ability to focus will be significantly affected and the risk of injury increases. Take at least one day of complete rest per week and limit your sessions to no more than an hour in length.

Inadequate warm-up

The warm-up is essential in staying injury free. If your warm-up is too short you are not fully prepared for the demands of your workout. Asking your body to apply a maximal force before it is properly warmed up, significantly increases the risk of injury. Follow the guidelines for warming up the previous page to make sure you are mentally and physically prepared for your workout.

Lack of concentration

If you're distracted or lackadaisical when training, your technique is more likely to deteriorate, which will increase your risk of injury. Develop your own mental checklist before each set, including checking that the weight and your body position is correct, and maintain your focus throughout each set.

Using a spotter and spotting techniques

There are certain occasions where having another person on hand to provide assistance, often called a spotter, is beneficial. If you are training at a high intensity there will be times where you won't be able to perform the last rep or two of a set. In certain exercises a spotter is required to safely return the weight to its starting position, including the squat and bench press.

Good spotting technique involves assisting the lifter to move the weight into the starting position and signalling that they now are in full control of the weight. For example, when lifting the weight off the rack in the bench press, the spotter will provide assistance and then might say 'your bar' as they take their hands away. As the lifter you should provide a clear signal that you can no longer lift the weight unaided and that you would like their assistance. You should agree on this signal before you start lifting.

The spotter should regard each rep as the last in a set and be ready to provide assistance as the lifter may encounter a problem at any time. At the end of the set the spotter may assist in returning the weight to the rack or the floor. This should be agreed beforehand so don't assume this is the case and pass the weight to the spotter expecting them to take it from you.

You needn't find the strongest person in the gym to spot for you. A spotter is only there if you find yourself struggling towards the end of a set and should provide minimal (a few kilograms) assistance. If your spotter is having to work harder than you are to help with the last few reps, the weight is too heavy.

Before you start each set explain to your spotter how many reps you are trying to do, whether you need any help lifting the weight into the starting position, and whether you want any assistance later in the set or them just to rack the weight if you are struggling.

A spotter can make heavy lifts much safer, as well as helping you to perform an extra rep or two at the end of a set which can help to increase the level of overload experienced. Spotters are most commonly used in free weights exercises but can also be of benefit with resistance machines, helping the lifter to move the weight into the starting position (the lowering phase) and assisting with the last couple of reps if required.

Clothing and footwear

The most important considerations for training clothing are that it should be comfortable and not restrict your movement. If you wear tight clothes it may constrict your movement and prevent a full range of motion. Close-fitting clothing may help you to better see your body position and check your technique, whilst very baggy clothing may get caught between weights or in resistance machines.

Your choice of footwear isn't as crucial as in other modes of exercise but should still be comfortable and supportive. A cross training shoe works well for weight training. If you become more serious you may consider purchasing special shoes for squats or deadlifts, or even a special shirt designed to increase your bench pressing ability. These are only really of significant use to those training for weightlifting competitions and offer little benefit to the recreational weight trainer.

Summing Up

- Stretching should form part of your routine in order to prevent injury and make your training more effective.

- Various strengthening exercises for the small muscles can help reduce the likelihood of an injury occurring.

- Your warm-up should include some mobility exercises, a pulse raiser, and light warm-up sets of the exercises in your programme.

- The most common causes of injury are using too much weight, incorrect technique, training too often, insufficient warm-up, and lack of concentration.

- Using a spotter can reduce the chances of an injury in some exercises and also help you complete an extra repetition or two at the end of a set.

- Your clothing should be comfortable and not restrict your movement. Cross training shoes are best for weight training.

Help List

About.com guide to Weight Training

www.weighttraining.about.com
Free information resource for weight training covering a number of topics related to weight training.

British Weightlifting Association

www.britishweightlifting.org
National organisation overseeing the administration of weightlifting clubs and competitions in the UK.

Great Britain Powerlifting Federation

www.gbpf.org.uk
National organisation responsible for the administration of powerlifting clubs and competitions in the UK.

My Protein

www.myprotein.com
Sports supplement manufacturer offering a wide range of products at excellent value.

National Strength and Conditioning Association

www.nsca-lift.org/perform
Bi-monthly e-journal covering a range of weightlifting and strength training topics.

Physical Company

www.physicalcompany.co.uk
Online suppliers of health and fitness equipment.

Pullum Sports

www.pullum-sports.co.uk
Online store specialising in weightlifting equipment and accessories.

Register of Exercise Professionals (REPs)

www.exerciseregister.org

The governing body for fitness in the UK, REPs safeguards those who use the services of fitness providers in the UK. Use the website to find accredited trainers, or courses to become a gym instructor or personal trainer.

Weight Loss Resources

www.weightlossresources.co.uk

A wealth of information about weight loss and training can be found on this website

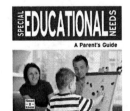

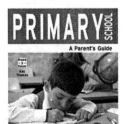

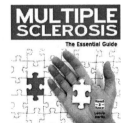